Forgiveness Inc.

Secret Spirituality at Work

SCOTT KRAJCA

ISBN: 978-1-4834-4172-6 (sc)
ISBN: 978-1-4834-4171-9 (e)

Library of Congress Control Number: 2015918631

wide Awake Publishing rev. date: 11/30/2015

This book is for *A Course in Miracles* students as well as spiritually-minded folks who want to live their spirituality and feel more peace, joy, and happiness (especially at a day job). Many thanks to the masters in our lives who remind us every day what true love and forgiveness are all about.

Much love to my wife, Mary, for her help and who is also the master in my life.

Special thanks to Deborah Roberts from the Foundation for Inner Peace for her guidance and help with the manuscript.

To my great friend and co-host on 'Of Course Radio', Sheldon Jo, who reminds me of what it's like to live the Course, to love and to practice forgiveness even when it may appear to be difficult.

"This is a course in mind training." T-1.VII.4:1.

CONTENTS

Introduction ix

CHAPTER I   What Is *A Course in Miracles?* 1

CHAPTER 2   What to Expect 7

CHAPTER 3   Life Lessons 13

CHAPTER 4   Metaphysics of *A Course in Miracles* 19

CHAPTER 5   The Text and Workbook 27

CHAPTER 6   Practicing Forgiveness at Work 31

CHAPTER 7   The Holy Spirit at Work 39

CHAPTER 8   Examples of Magical Results 45

CHAPTER 9   Workplace as a Mastery School 51

CHAPTER 10   Why Is This So Hard? 55

CHAPTER 11   Parting Thoughts 57

APPENDIX A   Course Resources 61

APPENDIX B   Forgiveness Thought Systems to Use at Work 63

Bibliography 67

Is it possible to be *spiritual* at a corporate job or at work? Can you live a life of mastery while you are also in a team meeting? Is there room for love in corporations?

If you're like me, I used to ask these questions and wonder what it would be like to live a life of spiritual mastery and get paid for it. The funny thing is I used to wall off my corporate experience and my spirituality. After I discovered the path of true forgiveness, I finally started experiencing the two merging together, and I can say that (internally) my experience is filled with more peace and happiness than I could ever imagine. And it all comes down to the discovery of *A Course in Miracles* (the Course) and the practice of true forgiveness. Because of this discovery, I have enjoyed secret spirituality while working at my day job.

I was originally introduced to *A Course in Miracles* after an intuitive reading in Sedona, Arizona, at the Center for New Age in 2005. The intuitive recommended that I buy a copy of the Course and begin studying it. I had no idea how influential this volume of information would be in my life. Truth be told, I opened the book a couple of times, found it hard to follow, and set it down for a couple of years.

Eventually the dark blue book with the gold lettering kept calling to me, and I found myself picking it up from time to time; however, I still found it hard to read continuously. I was on a concentrated spiritual path and was soaking in everything that came my way, especially if loved ones recommended something.

One day in 2006, a good friend recommended that I read a book that was about the Course and involved conversations with ascended masters. *The Disappearance of the Universe* by Gary Renard was the key to unlocking the door blocking my understanding of the Course (like it did for so many others). I was able to read the Text and finally practice the Workbook for Students all the way through the 365 lessons. I was even prodded into leading *A Course in Miracles* study group in San Mateo, California, in 2008. There I met so many incredible Course students and friends, including my great friend Sheldon Jo, who teaches me more about practicing forgiveness and love at work than anyone I know.

Today I am actively using *A Course in Miracles* at my day job. I have experienced some amazing transformations and have seen others change as well. The healing nature of the Holy Spirit and His ability to release guilt and fear from the mind is astounding.

I also see the challenges that each one of us faces, including myself, as we get caught up in personality and ego.

But just like learning to play an instrument or learning a new trade/hobby, the reality is that it takes time to reach a perfect state of Wholeness and Atonement. As *A Course in Miracles* says, "When we are ready, God Himself will take the final step in our return to Him." (Preface, pg. xiii).

I can openly admit that I seem to take two steps forward and one step back when it comes to remembering and applying what I have learned from the Course. Sometimes I feel like I have a strong relationship with Holy Spirit, and some days I am so caught up in my *stuff* that I forget it all and give in to thinking I am surrounded by bodies that I judge and condemn.

I say all of this for a few reasons, including the following:

1. One of the things the Course (Holy Spirit) asks us to do is to not hide anything as we go through the process. Just be honest with yourself, and don't condemn yourself for the mistakes you make along the way.
2. The process of self-judgment/self-deception while practicing the Course will definitely be there. It just may be more buried for some as opposed to others. But learning to not judge yourself and staying curious will be of great benefit to you along the journey.

3. Since time is illusory, why be concerned about how long it will take to finish the Course? Time is of the mind which means you are in control of your perception of time.

The workplace is our classroom for learning how to apply the concepts of the Course and to practice true forgiveness and see spirit in our brothers and sisters. I am very passionate about reframing our perspectives on our careers. Internally I remind myself that my main job is not building airplanes but practicing forgiveness, being happy and seeing love. Everything else is secondary.

Practicing the Course may be a simple concept, but it's not quite as easy to put into practice. We appear to be walking and talking in a world of duality, constantly forgetting we are really nestled at Home in Oneness with God. No matter what we appear to see with our eyes or hear with our ears, it's all just a trick to distract us from our real experience in Heaven.

A Course in Miracles is a course in training the mind. This is the true Jedi knight path to undo the ego and remember who you really are and where you really are. Everything else is simply smoke and mirrors created by the part of you that identifies with the ego, which was created at the point of separation.

When you understand the basic metaphysics of the Course (which we will go into more detail later), you basically understand that the ego mind was created after you separated from reality and went to sleep. God is still God, loving and extending. Our ego fell asleep to this, and in fact it has such fear of separating from God that the ego fractured and projects itself as galaxies, planets, people, animals, etc. Our job is to remember that God did not create anything that can die or change or make us feel bad. We must also enlist the help of the Holy Spirit to heal all of these separation thoughts in our mind. It's no surprise that the Holy Spirit is mentioned almost eight hundred times throughout the Course.

The aim of this book is to help guide those interested in reducing stress at work, reconnecting with Spirit and God, and realizing true happiness in their lives despite the silliness or wars that may be going on around you at work or home. Work environments vary, but my guess is that corporate life is fairly similar among individuals. Most people have a lot of responsibilities, deadlines, coworkers at various levels to deal with, and many opportunities for stress. What would it be like to glide through your day and be happy?

The Course strives to remind you of what you really are, where you really are, and who you really are. It employs many practical methods and useful tools that will allow you to one day live in a permanent place of remembrance of your place in heaven, a place of permanent peace. Sounds pretty darn good! And what better way to truly forgive and get there than to practice the Course every day of your life, especially at work, where there are so many opportunities to see your brothers and sisters as spirit?

The Course is simply one thought system and tool to get you to that place of happiness, joy, and peace. There are many other approaches, and by no means am I saying that *A Course in Miracles* is the only way to go. I have met people in my life who have definitely mastered certain areas of being in this world, and they all have different backgrounds, beliefs, and practices. I want to honor any person's path, especially since the end goal is the same.

Hopefully you can rest easy in the knowledge that there are others in the workplace that also have the same struggles or desires to be at peace at work. The corporate culture has done a good job of removing the heart and spirit from our daily work environment. Sure, there are exceptions to that statement, and if you're one of those people, it's nice to know that the happy dream is alive and well in some companies!

One of the great aspects of practicing the Course is that it is meant to be done on your own. It is an internal process that need not be shared with those around you (unless you feel encouraged to do so). True forgiveness is not about going to a colleague and saying something like, "You know you're an angry jerk, but I practice *A Course in Miracles*, so I forgive you." As the Holy Spirit might say, "You're just buying into the fact that you are seeing a separate, jerky body and simply projecting your subconscious guilt onto them."

The beauty of practicing the Course is that you are forgiving within your own mind. The goal is to lovingly see your colleagues, bosses, executives, board members, customers, and suppliers as your brothers and sisters in spirit. I will get into these details later in the book.

"Forgiveness, on the other hand, is still, and quietly does nothing. It offends no aspect of reality, nor seeks to twist it to appearances it likes. It merely looks, and waits, and judges not" (W-pII.1.4:1-3).

First, we will explore what the Course is and then examine what to expect from this book. At the end of the book, you will also find some helpful resources related to the Course and forgiveness thought systems/practices that you can use on a daily basis.

Also take note if any of the words used within the Course or this Text bring up any fears, apprehension, or even disgust. I grew up in a Catholic environment and had to "forgive" some of the words used in the Course (e.g., Holy Spirit, Atonement, forgive, and even the word God). It is easy to carry forward old programming, beliefs or biases. I would recommend working with Spirit and just letting go of any misgivings around certain words. Allow healing to occur or even simply replace some of the words for now so that you may progress.

Along the way, may you enjoy your journey and feel the benefits of true forgiveness! I also highly recommend that you grab your own copy of *A Course in Miracles* and put forgiveness into practice, especially while you are reading this book.

CHAPTER 1

What Is *A Course in Miracles?*

W hat is *A Course in Miracles?* What better way to answer the question than to start with a few quotes directly from the Course. "This is a course in mind training" (T-1.VII.4:1). "This is a course in how to know yourself" (T-16.III.4:1). "This is a course in cause and not effect" (T-21.VII.7:8).

These few simple statements say quite a bit about what *A Course in Miracles* is about. The fact that the Course is focused on "mind training" is a big clue as to how you can approach working with the Course. Mind training implies that this Course has nothing to do with letting people know about what the Course is or setting you up to "preach the gospel." This is meant to be a very personal journey. This is followed by the second quote that reaffirms how personal of a journey it will be—a course in knowing yourself. From the get-go this will either deeply intrigue or really scare folks. It also implies that this is not like typical religious doctrine and diatribes supporting the need to either preach or judge others along the way.

The focus on cause v. effect is the reason why the Course has been noted as a way to cut the time down considerably on the road to enlightenment. Even though the Course may talk in dualistic terms and metaphors, there is a clear focus on redirecting the student to a non-dualistic thought system and perception of reality. It does not address effects of projected guilt and fear but rather keeps directing the student back to the cause of his or her suffering and the resolution of healing the mind by practicing true forgiveness.

For example, the Course will remind you that if you feel unhappy at work, it's not because you didn't get a good promotion. It has to do with deep and/or buried sense of fear and guilt you hold for initially separating from God.

The Course's main aim is to correct your thinking and perception of reality. As stated in the introduction, "This course can therefore be summed up very simply in this way: *Nothing real can be threatened. Nothing unreal exists. Herein lies the peace of God*" (T-in.2:1–4).

Very simple statements like this one begin to introduce the student to a new way of considering reality. It sets the stage for some of the major concepts of the Course that I think many people struggle with. It hints at concepts of the ego, right v. wrong thinking, and ego v. God's creation.

The ego is mentioned almost nine hundred times throughout all of the material. Part of the mind training and application of practicing true forgiveness lies in understanding when you are siding with the ego as opposed to the Holy Spirit/God.

Many people also want to know more about the *miracles* within *A Course in Miracles*. Once again, let's look at some quotes from the Course.

- "Miracles are thoughts" (T-1.I.12:1).
- "Miracles are expressions of love, but they may not always have observable effects" (T-1.I.35:1).
- "The Holy Spirit is the mechanism of miracles. He recognizes both God's creations and your illusions. He separates the true from the false by His ability to perceive totally rather than selectively" (T-1.I.38:1–3).
- "The miracle forgives; the ego damns" (C-2.10:1).

These are just a few examples of the many different ways the Course describes miracles. But, to me, these explanations stand out. Once again, there is confirmation that the Course works at the mind level by stating that miracles are thoughts.

There is also a strong connection of love with miracles. The Course's interpretation of love is the unconditional kind (love just for the sake of loving with no expectations or love as extension with no expectations).

The Holy Spirit is your working partner throughout the Course and the application of the Course's principles. I also have to admit that I felt uncomfortable for a good couple of years whenever I would read the words *Holy Spirit*. There is some interesting programming that I had acquired growing up as a disgruntled Catholic that really surprised me. In fact, to this day I am still learning and growing my relationship with the Holy Spirit because of strange associations I made with this concept as an adolescent.

I have heard similar statements from other people as well. Some of the reasons we have a hard time following through with the Course involve the strong use of stereotypical Christian terms. For those who initially flinch at words like Holy Spirit, God, atonement, salvation, Christ, among other similar terms, I would just recommend sticking with the material and making peace with what these words might have meant to you in the past. That's another good forgiveness exercise!

The last of the previous quotes shows a clear distinction between a miracle (right-minded thinking) and the ego (wrong-minded thinking). The miracle will forgive while the ego will damn (condemn, judge, project, etc.).

Forgiveness is the powerful practice that the Course is asking you to undertake as your main job. So even if you're a _____ (fill in the blank) at your day job, your real job is to practice forgiveness.

So what is forgiveness from the Course's perspective? Once again, let's go to the Course for answers.

– "Forgiveness recognizes what you thought your brother did to you has not occurred. It does not pardon sins and make them real. It sees there was no sin. And in that view are all your sins forgiven. What is sin, except a false idea about God's Son? Forgiveness merely sees its falsity, and therefore lets it go. What then is free to take its place is now the Will of God" (W-pII.1:1–7).

- "Miracle-minded forgiveness is only correction. It has no element of judgment at all. The statement 'Father forgive them for they know not what they do' in no way evaluates what they do. It is an appeal to God to heal their minds" (T-2.V.16:1–4).
- "Forgiveness is the healing of the perception of separation. Correct perception of your brother is necessary, because minds have chosen to see themselves as separate. Spirit knows God completely. That is its miraculous power" (T-3.V.9:1–4).

In brief, forgiveness is about reminding yourself that what you think you see with your eyes is not true. Everything you see around you is typically interpreted by your egoic mind as a sign of separateness from yourself and from God. Forgiveness is all about remembering that you are not separate from God, your brothers and sisters are not separate from God, and our true state is spirit.

This again is why the Course stresses working with the Holy Spirit to help forgive and heal your mind. The Holy Spirit's mind is still joined with God, while your ego mind is split and typically sides with fear and guilt by making everything outside of God real.

For example, when you get upset by a colleague showing up late or not following through, you make this reality more real and side with the ego. When you judge other colleagues or coworkers and see them as something other than spirit, you are siding with the ego. The goal is to think with the Holy Spirit and see everyone with love and view all as spirit. When you are having difficulty doing this, hand it over to the Holy Spirit to help heal your mind and put you at peace.

Start developing a personal relationship with God and the Holy Spirit today (if you haven't already). This is the pure relationship that will move your mind out of fear and guilt and into a life of peace, happiness, and joy. Some folks like to speak or pray to the Holy Spirit with the use of a symbol (like Jesus Christ or another ascended master with whom they feel a connection).

For me, I tend to connect to the Holy Spirit as a feeling in my heart.

Lately I have felt the urge to connect to the ascended master Mary Magdalene (which is a whole other discussion).

I will get more into the metaphysics of the Course a bit later in the book, but for now, let's look at how the Course is broken down.

The bulk of the Course is the Text section. This is where all of the concepts described above (and much more) are laid out. The Course is all about repeating the same things over and over but from slightly different perspectives. This is done to address the different aspects of the separated mind (ego). I am still astounded at how I am able to pick up new information and understanding of the Course every time I read it.

As you practice forgiveness, you will see the meaning of the Course and its words in a new light. The Text is meant to explain

- miracles;
- the separation;
- the roles of the ego, fear, guilt, and the body;
- the role of the Holy Spirit;
- God's plan through atonement, holy instant, and salvation;
- forgiveness;
- healing and correction; and
- peace.

Another powerful section of the Course is the Workbook for Students. The Workbook is set up to be a daily practice for one year, and it is intended to get you to think with the Holy Spirit and practice forgiveness on a daily basis. For many beginners this seems like a daunting task. I cannot count how many times I resisted starting (and continuing) the Workbook. For most people it takes longer than a year to complete. What I can say is that if you stick with it, the lessons get easier and easier. I remember transitioning from a place of near dread to sheer excitement and enjoyment for the lesson of the day. This is all symbolic of how the ego really does not want you to practice forgiveness at all.

I cannot stress enough how important doing all 365 lessons from the Workbook can be, especially while you are at a day job. The lessons are set up so that you can practice them quietly within your own mind. Later in the book, I will offer suggestions on how you can practice the lessons at work.

The last two sections of the Course include the Manual for Teachers and the Clarification of Terms. The Manual for Teachers was written because it is used as a "frequently asked questions" section. The Holy Spirit anticipated the types of questions that Course students would have and then answered them in the third section of the book. I also like how this section goes into more explanation of how to put *A Course in Miracles* into practice on a daily basis.

The Clarification of Terms section is great since it condenses a lot of the terminology and concepts discussed in the Text.

Lastly, let's briefly discuss who wrote the Course and when. A great resource for more information on the scribing and history of the Course can be found at the Foundation for Inner Peace's website (www.acim.org).

The Course was scribed by Helen Schucman, PhD, who was an associate professor of medical psychology at Columbia-Presbyterian Medical Center in New York City. Helen worked with Bill Thetford, PhD, but they had strong personality conflict issues. Bill suggested that there had to be a better way for them to work together, and Helen agreed. Shortly after this agreement, Helen began having psychic and spiritual experiences. This eventually led to her hearing a very distinct voice that she would later find out was the voice of Jesus/Holy Spirit. On October 21, 1965, she heard the following words: "This is *A Course in Miracles*. Please take notes."[1] And the rest is history—

---

[1] Foundation for Inner Peace, http://acim.org/Scribing/about_scribes.html

CHAPTER 2

What to Expect

While you are practicing forgiveness, there are several things that you should and most likely should not expect. Let's take the time to go through some assumptions you may have or some that I had before beginning the journey of practicing secret spirituality at work.

First off, practicing forgiveness is simple but not easy. You will probably have days when you feel peaceful, when you are practicing the Course in a masterful way, and when you actually see events or people around you changing. There will also be plenty of days when you will get sucked into the ego's version of your reality and will feel upset and out of sorts. You may even want to give up.

I know I had some expectations that as I practiced the Course, everything around me would get better. The people I interacted with would become more spiritually-minded. I would encounter fewer conflicts, and my life would be an easy flow of peace and love. That couldn't be further from the truth.

While I have had some really amazing experiences and basically feel a lot better about my work situation, I still have to deal with a lot of chaos and unhappy people. But I can say that I feel a whole lot better about things no matter what might be happening around me.

So here is a quick list of things that you can reasonably expect while you are practicing *A Course in Miracles* at work.

- It takes a lot of practice to think with the Holy Spirit, and you will probably need to set up reminders around the office or your desk to help you remember what your real job is.

- Your relationships with colleagues and coworkers *will* change, but they may not always change the way you would intend from your singular perspective.
- You will feel more peaceful and happy the more you release guilt and fear by using work situations and coworkers to practice forgiveness.
- Doing the Workbook lessons at work is possible, and it's a great way to practice forgiveness in a work setting.
- Miracles will show up in ways you could never predict or expect.
- You will establish a closer relationship with God, the Holy Spirit, Jesus Christ, and/or other ascended symbols.

It's important to point out that while you may experience personal peace and happiness as you practice the Course, you must still deal with the separated ego. Some folks just won't respond well to peace and happiness. Two of the classic ego reactions include projecting and attacking. You may be the perfect projection symbol for someone's ego to attack, and that person may go after you to ease his or her own sense of guilt. For example, you may feel very peaceful and help a work team resolve conflict, but in the process of offering help you could become the target of attack or ridicule. This type of experience would be just another opportunity to practice forgiveness. Sometimes that's easier said than done.

I should also point out that as you practice forgiveness and allow the Holy Spirit to heal your mind, there may be some wonderful surprises in the way of miracles. Relationships may actually heal. Or that boss that was really hard on you may start to lighten up. Or that really difficult coworker may take another job in a completely different division. Who knows what may happen. But having a dualistic experience also means that you will experience what appears to be *good* or *bad* experiences throughout your life. So just go about doing your main job—forgiveness. Allow your mind to heal so that no matter what you are presented in life, your response will always be from a place of peace and love.

The process of practicing the Course involves a lot of help from the Holy Spirit. You are not alone, and the Holy Spirit is actually the one doing all of the work. You are simply handing over all of your problems, your issues, or your lack of peace to the Holy Spirit. I will detail this relationship later in the book.

Here are some things that you should *not* expect while you are practicing *A Course in Miracles* at work.

- Colleagues or coworkers noticing that you are always forgiving at work.
- A change in your basic personality.
- *Everyone* around you becoming more peaceful and easier to work with.
- Work situations are always easier.
- All of your relationships heal.
- Getting that raise/promotion or any other form of material expectation.

The key is to be vigilant of your thoughts and practice a lot, especially at the beginning of the process. That's not to say amazing and miraculous things will not or may not happen, but I think it's best to not play into another trick of the ego by expecting a lot of things to shift external to your own inner experience. You may also practice forgiveness, and your external world/relationships may still seem to get worse. It's simply another opportunity to forgive them. But it could also be an opportunity for you to ask for guidance and decide if you must leave the situation. There's no need for anyone else to carry the cross like Jesus did. He's been there and done that for us!

For me, I went through a couple of years of very stressful situations at work. I was a manager at a time in our company when several high-level decisions were causing a lot of grief for the working-level team members. I was practicing the Course, but I still felt stress and anxiety around executing projects and performing my daily management role.

By the end of the two years, I consulted internally about transitioning out of management and back into an engineering role. In the past I had left situations too soon and noticed I would have to repeat lessons later, and they were usually more intense after that. This time I wanted to check in with Spirit and make sure that I wasn't running away. I felt that wasn't the case and that I would still be afforded all of the wonderful forgiveness opportunities regardless of my role.

After the transition out of management, I still had plenty of forgiveness opportunities, but I can see that I personally enjoy my work situation a lot more now. I see that my passion is centered around technical issues, not managerial issues but I would still act as a leader on projects. I also see how much I have grown because of my past experiences, but there was no need to carry the cross anymore.

I also want to caution anyone who thinks the Course is about manifesting material things. I have run into some folks in the past who confuse the message of the Course with the law of attraction or manifesting tools. The Course is pretty clear that the aim is to realize we are not bodies, but spirit, and applying some of the ideas from the Course to *manifest* is clearly missing the point.

I can see where folks may be confused. The Course clearly states that our minds are powerful and that we create what we hold in our minds. But we need to keep in mind that the aim of the Course is to direct our minds to God, love, Spirit, but nothing else (if we want to transcend our ego and karma in a shorter amount of time).

The previous statements are not meant to vilify anyone on a path to practice the law of attraction. Anything we pursue in bodies will bring up opportunities to forgive and remember who we really are and who our brothers and sisters really are. While you are on the path to attract millions of dollars (or whatever your desire is), you will most certainly be given plenty of forgiveness opportunities (i.e., disappointments, interesting characters, difficult choices, doubts, etc.).

Some other things that *may* occur as you practice the Course at work include the following:

-   increased intuitive abilities,
-   healed relationships,
-   people wanting to know more about your *secret* for staying so calm, peaceful, and happy,
-   surprising conversations with people you would least expect,
-   flashes of light out of the corner of your eyes,
-   overwhelming sense of oneness or connection,
-   sense of your body fading away,
-   spiritual/psychic vision,
-   remaining peaceful in situations where others are clearly stressed out,
-   enjoying others successes, and
-   desiring opportunities you previously perceived as difficult.

I've listed the items outlined here based on either my own personal experiences or what I have heard from friends who practice the Course in their work environment.

Since the Course is a personal journey, each person will most likely discover unique experiences that may not have been discussed in this section. Positive or negative, the external experiences are all meant to function as tools for forgiveness so that you can remember who and where you really are.

Life Lessons

In order to tell my story, I need to start a couple of years before I bought my first copy of *A Course in Miracles*. I was in my late twenties. I had a corporate job and worked as an engineer. I was living in downtown Seattle, and I was working at a place and in a position where I should have been really happy. But in actuality, I was miserable. I sort of knew I was miserable, but I didn't know enough to really do anything about my situation.

One day in 2003, I came home from work, turned on the TV, popped open a beer, and just zoned out. At one point I became very much aware of thoughts zooming around my mind that I did not like at all. I was hearing myself think, *You're no good. No one wants to date you. You're not as far in your career as you should be. You suck.* Nice, huh?

I sat in stunned realization for a few seconds, observing all of these thoughts fly around inside my mind. I then turned off the TV and just sat in silence. It was definitely a life-changing moment, one that would put me on a path to eventual happiness. But it certainly was a journey.

I immediately got rid of my cable box and felt completely liberated by my newfound silent lifestyle while I was at home. I had grown up Catholic, but I had heard of New Age folks meditating, so I decided to try it on my own. When I would meditate, I started to get sensations that used to scare me. I would start to get quiet, and it would feel like I wanted to leave my body. I started to play around with this rather than give in to my fear of it, and eventually I noticed that it felt like I popped out of my body and floated several feet above myself. It felt like I was a balloon on a tether. Once I relaxed into the sensation, the fear went away, and I felt really safe. Eventually I would meditate and not feel the need to pop out of my body.

I had also broken up with a nice gal around this time, and I think she was also concerned about my state of mind. She didn't know I had started meditating, but she got me to try out a life coach she was seeing named Robin. I called Robin up and found an immediate connection and really liked what she was offering. This was an opportunity to focus on myself and discover what it was I wanted out of life. I didn't really know what the process entailed, but at some level I knew I needed help.

After several months I felt like I had several breakthroughs. I realized that I was still living a life that I thought my parents wanted me to have. It wasn't what I wanted. I knew that there was more out there for me, and I was beginning to take the steps to find out. I wrote my first song. I started writing a novel. I wrote poems. I was starting to feel fulfilled, but I also knew there were more substantial things I wanted. Spirituality interested me, but I was still confused. I wondered, *Am I an atheist or what?*

As a side note, I had survived a plane crash (along with my two younger cousins) when I was nineteen. This experience left me with deep unanswered questions about God and the meaning of life, and I went through a phase in which I felt angry with God for several years.

I clearly remember having a life coaching session one day, and I felt some physical pain in my heart. Robin offered to send me Reiki, and I had this weird/automatic response. I immediately said, "No!" It was strange to watch. A part of me really wanted to experience it. I also noticed this about my personality. Typically I would say no to things I really wanted as a way of punishing myself. What a great lesson in ego!

Eventually I said yes to Reiki, and it was another life-changing moment. I really enjoyed it. I also met my next girlfriend a few months later, and that was one of her first questions. "Have you ever heard of Reiki?" I was blown away!

I was also lucky that I met a woman who was really into spiritual concepts, and that opened the door for a lot of my exposure to

Buddhism, Hinduism, New Age philosophy, metaphysics, and more. I devoured all kinds of books. I went to meditation classes. I tried yoga (definitely not for me). I received Reiki initiations. I also remember a time when we went down to Olympia, Washington, to see a traveling display of the remains of a Buddhist monk who was enlightened (based on pearls remaining behind with his skeleton). When I got close to the display, my head started buzzing like crazy! It was such a fun experience, and it only left me wanting more in the ways of understanding spirituality.

In my next relationship, I was further immersed in more New Age exposure, and I was very grateful. By that time I had taken Reiki training and had become a Reiki master. I had also taken Matrix Energetics classes, and I enjoyed giving hands on healing sessions for people.

And yet I still felt some sort of emptiness. I was still looking for answers. *Why are we here? What's the point to all of this? Who am I?* Those questions kept me going.

I actually remember the day I bought *A Course in Miracles*. I had just had a psychic reading in Sedona, Arizona, and someone recommended that I go downstairs to the bookstore and buy the Course and start reading/practicing it. I have to admit that when I got it home, I started thumbing through it and found it really hard to read. I would open various sections and read maybe a few sentences, and then I would have to put it down. A part of me really wanted to understand it better, and yet there was an equal part of my mind that just couldn't get into it.

Not too long after that, I quit my corporate job in hopes that I could become a full-time life coach after I was certified. I would eye the Course a lot and would occasionally pick the book up, but I couldn't bring myself to read it.

So it sat. It sat on my shelf until a friend of mine mentioned a book she just read that completely blew her away. It was entitled *The Disappearance of the Universe* (aka DU) by Gary Renard. That book and another experience not too long after that completely changed my life … again!

DU was completely incredible. It literally answered all of the questions I had rattling around in my mind. *Who are we? Where are we from?*

What's the point? What is A Course in Miracles, *and how do you practice it?* I finished *The Disappearance of the Universe* in short order. Being an engineer by training, I was also curious to conduct a test. I wanted to see what would happen if I tried reading the Course again.

When I started reading passages from the Course, it all started to make sense. I was able to follow the words without getting tired or wanting to put it down. I even started the Workbook (which would take me almost two years to complete).

A lot changed for me during that time. I finished Co-Active leadership training. I went to see Eli Jaxon-Bear at a Satsang (spiritual talk) in Vancouver, BC. It was one of the most incredible experiences I've had. Eli likes to use self-inquiry as a way to help people wake up and sends out the transmission of the silent mind. I remember him asking me what my thoughts were, and as I thought, my mind just stopped! I experienced this "lack of mind" all day. I was stunned and elated. I remember driving home that night and looking up at the stars while I was driving, but I still didn't experience thoughts. I just giggled with glee.

During this time I was still figuring out what kind of a business I was going to have. I had completed leadership training and started to consult for some small businesses.

A friend of mine had been interested in channeling and started to connect with higher self, which got me interested. Something kept prodding me to try it. Eventually I started channeling and had an amazing experience. I remember feeling this super tall body within mine, and it also felt like my fingers were twice as long. I was always very intentional with the channeling and wanted to make sure it was of high integrity. A lot of the messages that came through were very much like the material in *A Course in Miracles.*

I channeled for many months, doing readings for friends and anyone who wanted a reading. Eventually it led me to meet Darrin Owens (psychic and author), and he convinced me to start to do intuitive readings at a metaphysical bookstore in San Mateo, California. Darrin was also the catalyst to have me lead a Course study group through the metaphysical bookstore.

In short order, we had a pretty core group of folks who would come every week. We were all experiencing strong connections to the Course material, and people were starting to have some pretty amazing personal experiences. I was in a state of bliss and felt like I was at home. I met people who became very close friends, including my dearest friend, Sheldon Jo (now the co-host on Of Course Radio–a bi-weekly BBS Radio program focused on *A Course in Miracles*).

But the Holy Spirit had other plans for me. I lost all of my consulting clients within couple of weeks and I was even asked to leave the apartment where I was living.. The Course folks helped me out while I decided I should go back to work at my corporate job in Seattle.

I always seemed to have this knack for doing things twice, so I figured I needed to go back to a corporate job and really practice forgiveness and leave my blissful community behind.

This book (for me) is really about knuckling down and applying spirituality/forgiveness at work based on coming back into a corporate job. It's about learning to love something I previously disliked and had judgments around.

I remember my first day back as an engineer. I still had the blissful glow about me. I walked right into a group of pretty negative engineers that were complaining about the shop workers who were on strike. All of my memories of working in a corporation came crashing in at once, and my bliss bubble started to burst.

Over several years I worked as an engineer and then eventually got into management, all the while knowing my opportunities for practicing forgiveness were increasing at an exponential rate. As a manager, I went through an intense round of forgiveness opportunities and experienced that I could get through tough times by practicing forgiveness (I will discuss more in later chapters). Now back as an engineer, I can enjoy my work as well as practice forgiveness with a lot more ease. Recent challenges seem insignificant to the challenges I faced in the two years as a manager.

I wouldn't say I was completely graceful along the way, but after I encountered some very stressful and tense situations with colleagues, other managers, and direct reports, I am finally able to see and feel the effects of practicing forgiveness. It was a lot of hard work, and there were times when I thought I was going crazy (my poor wife); however, in the end it was so worth it!

I decided to write about my spiritual path because I had heard many similar stories from other folks and I thought it was good to show people that we share common threads. I also feel it's important for all of us to share our personal journeys, especially if they can offer practical insight to the good things and the challenges we all may encounter along the way. It's nice to know that even though sometimes we may seem alone in our journeys, others are really walking beside us or may have paved the way in front of us at times.

I am looking forward to continuing to apply forgiveness at work and eagerly look forward to the next set of challenges.

CHAPTER 4

Metaphysics of *A Course in Miracles*

Again, I will be using quotes from the Course to help explain some of the metaphysics, but quite honestly I would also recommend checking out some of the metaphysics material presented by Ken Wapnick at the Foundation for *A Course in Miracles*. Ken transitioned out of his body in 2014, but his outstanding material is still available at the Foundation's website (http://facim.org/bookstore).

I would also highly recommend reading all of the Gary Renard books. *The Disappearance of the Universe* has excellent explanations of the metaphysics of the Course throughout as shared by the ascended masters Arten and Pursah. His other books include *Your Immortal Reality* and *Love Has Forgotten No One*.

For a discussion on Course metaphysics, let's start with the following quotes from *A Course in Miracles*:

- "Your ego is never at stake because God did not create it. Your spirit is never at stake because He did" (T-4.I.7:8–9).
- "God did not make the body, because it is destructible, and therefore not of the Kingdom" (T-6.V.A.2:1).
- "The world you see is an illusion of a world. God did not create it, for what He creates must be eternal as Himself. Yet there is nothing in the world you see that will endure forever. Some things will last in time a little while longer than others. But the time will come when all things visible will have an end" (C-4.1:1–5).
- "Lesson 14—God did not create a meaningless world. God did not create it, and so it is not real. Say, for example: God did not

create that war, and so it is not real. God did not create that airplane crash, and so it is not real" (W-pI.14.4:3–6).

One thing that's very evident from the previous quotes is that God did not have a hand in creating our bodies, our egos, or the world we see with our physical eyes. This statement alone is enough to greatly confuse most people.

We have all been taught from the Bible that God created the heavens and the earth, that God created Adam and Eve, and that God has a hand in all of the good and bad things that occur on the earth and in our experiences. The Course flatly refutes that position by openly stating that God did not create anything that is not eternal and of love.

The ego is responsible for creating all of the things we see with our physical eyes, anything that appears separate and anything that is not permanent.

The Course simply looks at the world we live in as an illusion and a reflection of our separated mind creating apart from God/Source. The real truth is that we are still in heaven with God, but somehow we have fallen asleep to this truth.

The Course calls this *the separation*. From the Course's perspective, we created the separation by believing in *mad ideas* and thinking we can create separate from God.[2]

At some point an aspect of God decided (or thought or imagined) that it could create apart from God. At that point a true separation occurred. It is also known as the "deep sleep." This separated aspect fell asleep to God's grace and love. In fact, the Course also links this initial separation to the source of fear and guilt that we suffer from whenever we side with the ego. Fear and guilt are what run the ego.

Again, I think *The Disappearance of the Universe* has one of the best explanations of what happened at the time of separation in chapter 4, "The Secrets of Existence."

Basically, an aspect of God wondered what it would be like to

---

[2] *A Course in Miracles*, T-2.I.1:9–12.

create apart from God, and then *bang!* it got exactly what it thought, namely an existence outside of God. This existence created great fear, since God does not respond to anything that is not of Itself. So the only response this separated thought had was to experience fear and "run away." It ran within its own creations and created what we know as the universe (or the multiverse if you're so inclined). The ego continuously lives in fear and guilt for what it thinks it did. It continuously creates more separated versions so it does not have to return to the Source/God and be condemned. Of course, this is insane thinking.

In reality, we are just a collective aspect of God that has fallen asleep in a made-up nightmare, and God is patiently waiting for us to awaken to His love. God simply exists in eternal love, and that is exactly where we are, except we have forgotten it because we believe in the existence of bodies.

The Holy Spirit is the Voice of God placed gently in our nightmare, patiently acting as the return beacon home. The Holy Spirit was created at the moment of the separation to remind us of who and where we really are.

The Holy Spirit is here to heal our minds of the "tiny, mad idea"[3] that we are separated from God.

Forgiveness is simply our tool and the tool of the Holy Spirit to help us remember who and where we really are. It is meant to be the way we stop ourselves when we are judgmental, angry, upset, distraught, depressed, sad, etc. It is meant to heal all of the ways we project our guilt and fear outward or inward. The ego needs to project these things because it is so afraid to stop and look back to the moment of separation in fear of retribution from God, which will never come.

So as separated aspects of the one mind, it is each and every one of our jobs to practice love and forgiveness so that our whole mind can eventually be healed. This will lead to the eventual "disappearance of the universe" and a time when our single mind will wake back up with God.

---

[3] *A Course in Miracles*, T-25.I.5:5.

God did not create the universe. As shocking as it might seem at first, but if you sit with it for a bit, it starts to make sense. The whole concept that God would allow or want us to experience death, disease, violence, and evil just seems wrong. The fact that our splintered, fearful, and guilty egotistic mind has created all of these things can make a lot of sense.

It is also reassuring to know that we are truly safe and at home with God in heaven. If we keep remembering this, we will eventually experience this truth. And part of the way to remember this is to see your brothers and sisters as people who have this access as well.

This alone is a great motivator for practicing forgiveness, especially in environments where it may be more difficult to pause and remember who we really are (like in the workplace).

As the Course says in chapter 23 of the Text, we can rise above the battleground of the world. When you look down onto the chaotic mess the ego has made, you can make the choice for miracles instead of "murder."[4] This is part of the forgiveness process—to not be of the world but to look at it through the eyes of forgiveness.

Just understanding the metaphysical truth of our situation and forgiving with our own conscious minds is only part of the way out. Another big component to the metaphysical piece is the large role the Holy Spirit plays in healing our minds.

The Holy Spirit is known by many names in the Course, including the Healer, the Comforter, and the Guide.[5] There are many passages from the Course that help us understand the role and function of the Holy Spirit. Several that stand out include the following:

— "The Holy Spirit is in the part of the mind that lies between the ego and the spirit, mediating between them always in favor of the spirit" (T-7.IX.1:5).

---

[4] *A Course in Miracles*, T-23.IV.4 and T-23.IV.5.
[5] *A Course in Miracles*, T-5.I.4:2

- "The Holy Spirit will help you reinterpret everything that you perceive as fearful, and teach you that only what is loving is true" (T-5.IV.1:3).
- "Only the Holy Spirit can resolve conflict, because only the Holy Spirit is conflict-free" (T-6.II.11:8).
- "All healing is release from the past. That is why the Holy Spirit is the only Healer. He teaches that the past does not exist, a fact which belongs to the sphere of knowledge, and which therefore no one in the world can know" (T-13.VIII.1:1–3).
- "In your practice, try to give over every plan you have accepted for finding magnitude in littleness" (T-15.IV.4:5).

The key is that handing over your problems and issues to the Holy Spirit is a very important part of the forgiveness process. Basically the Course is asking you to start to develop a personal relationship with the Holy Spirit so that your vision and mind can be healed and corrected.

The Holy Spirit can do this for you because the mind of the Holy Spirit is still whole and intact with God. Yours is not. Our mind still identifies with the ego, and we cannot possibly know how to heal the mind; however, the Holy Spirit knows.

In summary, here is a breakdown of the metaphysics of the Course.

1. We are still at home with God, but at one point there was a tiny, mad idea to create separate from God.
2. At this thought about being separate, there was also an immense sense of fear and guilt.
3. In that brief moment of fear/guilt, the ego was created and began separating in order to hide, and our dualistic universe/reality was created.
4. At the same moment, the Holy Spirit formed as a bridge between our true home and our false home. The Holy Spirit is the gentle voice reminding us to awaken to our true reality.
5. Forgiveness is one tool to remember who we truly are and where we truly are with the help of the Holy Spirit.

From the Course, we can see a basic formula to follow whenever we need to forgive. When we say forgive, we are really talking about any thought, situation, judgment, or personal interaction that places us out of peace and love. But in order to forgive, there is a process.

> I must have decided wrongly, because I am not at peace. I made the decision myself, but I can also decide otherwise. I want to decide otherwise, because I want to be at peace. I do not feel guilty, because the Holy Spirit will undo all the consequences of my wrong decision if I will let Him. I choose to let Him, by allowing Him to decide for God for me. (T-5.VII.6:7–11)

The beauty of using forgiveness as a tool with the Holy Spirit is that you can work with it in past, present, or future states. You can think back to times that you have had great fear, guilt, anger, and judgment and follow the same process. You can understand that you are not at peace and that you have bought in to a false truth about either yourself or your brother/sister, and then you can hand the issue over to the Holy Spirit for healing.

One of the bigger pieces I also got out of Gary Renard's books is that we also need to remember that we hold accountability in our view of reality. Remembering that we created what we are seeing is a big piece to getting out of the ego trap.

For example, if someone appears to cut you off in traffic, it would be very easy to get upset and become angry with that person in a typical egoic mind-set. In reality, the collective conscious, you as the ego, created the situation to once again convince yourself that you are a separate body and that the other body deserves to be condemned and judged for the thing he or she did to you.

When you practice forgiveness, it will look something like this.

1. You catch yourself feeling angry or upset.
2. You become mindful to the fact that you are getting caught in a trap that you ultimately created with the ego.

3. You decide that you do not want to feel this way anymore.

4. You hand the matter over to the Holy Spirit for healing.

I will get into more detail on following the formula outlined here while we are at work in a later chapter.

Keeping the metaphysics of the Course in mind has been very helpful for me and for many other Course students. It helps create a shift in perception that will allow not only you but also your brothers and sisters to become whole again.

Here are some examples of how knowing the metaphysics of the Course can shift perception and create true healing.

Situation	Old Belief	Forgiveness Perspective
Someone cuts you off in traffic.	That person is wrong and deserves to be condemned and yelled at.	That person is my brother/sister, and I release any negative feelings or thoughts to Spirit.
A politician you do not like is on TV.	That guy/gal is an idiot, and so are the people who support him or her.	I may not agree with this person, but he or she is spirit (like me), whole and innocent.
You read or see on TV any number of violent news stories.	You say, "God, please help that person or those people. I hate how crazy this world is."	These images are exactly what the ego wants. My heart goes out to the people, and yet I know that we are all really in heaven with God. Holy Spirit, please heal these images.

Situation	Old Belief	Forgiveness Perspective
A coworker says something in a meeting that really upsets you.	You think they are stupid, rude, disrespectful, etc. You hope they get what's coming to them.	Look at them and drum up as much love as you can in your heart. In your mind, see them as white light or as spirit living in heaven.
Your boss or manager criticizes you or gives negative feedback, and you feel pretty bummed out.	You start to feel really depressed and allow negative thoughts to flood your mind, or you project anger outward and decide that this person is a real jerk.	In your mind, go back to the interaction, and instead of reacting, ask the Holy Spirit to come into the encounter and heal the exchange. Keep doing it until you feel peaceful about yourself and your boss.

The real trick is catching yourself every time you are not experiencing peace. The ego is very tricky, so it may take a lot of your personal attention to notice when you are caught up in the ego's frame of mind. The key is to not beat yourself up whenever you catch yourself. Just be gentle and remember to apply the forgiveness formula or to simply state that you would rather experience peace than whatever it is you are currently experiencing.

The other component to practicing secret spirituality at work is to look around and send love to your coworkers and work situations. If you replace your mind with love, then you will remember that you are love.

For more examples of using forgiveness thought systems in the workplace, please see appendix B.

CHAPTER 5

The Text and Workbook

Rather than discuss what the Text and the Workbook for Students sections are all about, this chapter will focus on how to use them as useful tools for practicing forgiveness.

One of the more common questions that new Course students ask is this: "Should I read the Text first or start on the Workbook lessons?"

I have heard several opinions on this, and I will also share my own experiences. But in the end, it's best to listen to your own guidance. You might experiment by starting to read the Text a little bit at a time or even randomly flipping through the Text to see if any sections pop out at you. Or maybe you're called to start the Workbook section immediately.

When it comes to the Workbook, there are some rules that the Course spells out, including the following:[6]

1. Do not do more than one lesson per day.
2. Practice the lessons with great specificity.
3. Do not decide for yourself that there are some people, situations, or things to which the ideas are inapplicable.

When I started working with the Course, I would randomly flip through the Text. I would look at the Workbook lessons, but somehow I knew I wasn't ready. After I read the *Disappearance of the Universe*, I started to read the Text and started doing the Workbook lessons at the same time. Eventually I completed the Text before I completed all of

---

[6] *A Course in Miracles*, W.Intro:10, 19–21.

the Workbook lessons (almost two years later). I then went back and reread the Text completely a second time and then did the Workbook lessons a second time (all in a calendar year). After I went through everything once, it was like a switch got turned on, and the material seemed to make more sense. Plus it was more interesting the second time through.

In today's world of technology, it is really handy to have a copy of *A Course in Miracles* saved on a smartphone or computer. Some folks may not feel comfortable having that beautiful blue book sitting on their desks or shelves at work.

You can download digital copies and have them available on smartphones or computers as either pdf files or through applications like Kindle. There are also smartphone apps available that are focused on capturing all of the Course or only the Workbook sections. I will list current applications and Course sources in the resources appendix of this book.

Regardless of the method, it is strongly recommended that you start your day by either connecting with the Course material or putting your thoughts toward God/the Holy Spirit.

I actually have the book at work and on my smartphone (via Kindle). While my computer is firing up in the morning, I will either read a random passage from the Text or look through one of the Workbook lessons.

If I am actively doing the yearlong Workbook lessons, I tend to use the lesson cards available through the Foundation for Inner Peace (http://shop.acim.org/products/lesson-cards). I keep them in my pocket throughout the workday. For some of the lessons, I would write the thought system on the back of my hand so that I could look at it throughout the day.

I have even seen people write *A Course in Miracles* quotes at the bottom of their e-mail auto signatures at work. As a side note, I asked one of the managers I worked with if she practiced the Course after I saw her quote. She said she didn't know what *A Course in Miracles* was but that she liked the quote. The Holy Spirit works in mysterious ways!

There are several quotes in the Course that do not reveal that it is a spiritual Text. If you do not feel comfortable broadcasting your affinity for the Course at work, I would recommend searching and pulling out quotes from the Text that may seem corporate-safe so that you can post them around your desk or on your computer. The more reminders you can set for yourself, the easier it will be to maintain a spiritual frame of mind.

There are a couple sections of the Text that would be worth reading either before work or during breaks at work. The first is titled "The Lessons of the Holy Spirit," which is located in chapter 6. These lessons will put you in a wonderfully spiritual frame of mind. Even reading the three main lesson topic headers can be enough (A, B, and C). "The Obstacles to Peace" in chapter 19 also has some really good reminders to help set your frame of mind while you are at work (in my opinion), especially section B and the discussion of the attraction of pain.

Just flipping randomly to quotes is probably one of the simplest and usually very timely ways of gleaning the most appropriate message for you in the moment. I cannot count how many times I have flipped the Course open and felt how the quote I read fit perfectly with what was going on in my personal situation.

CHAPTER 6

Practicing Forgiveness at Work

"Forgiveness is the healing of the perception of separation. Correct perception of your brother is necessary, because minds have chosen to see themselves as separate. Spirit knows God completely. That is its miraculous power" (T-3.V.9:1–4).

Once again, if you really want to wake up and remember your place of eternal bliss with God, then practicing forgiveness is your main job. Any job titles, tasks, project deadlines, finance goals, and reports need to take a backseat in a sense. I am in no way advocating that you slough off at work now that you're practicing forgiveness. I am only saying that your mind-set needs to be completely reframed the minute you wake up to the minute you go to sleep every day.

This may sound daunting, but if you really want to wake up in this lifetime, then your spiritual practice needs to be given attention everywhere your mind and body goes. Think of practicing the Course and forgiveness as a needed lifestyle change. Not like a diet, but a way to put on your happy coat every day and to see the world for what it truly is and allow your mind and the minds of those around you to heal.

There are a couple of important pieces to practicing forgiveness at work. One is to surround yourself with reminders that you are meant to practice forgiveness all day every day. Ways of doing that include reading portions of the Text throughout the day, practicing the Workbook, setting reminders for you to read, or pausing to connect with Holy Spirit (like setting a private meeting notice reminder every hour in your digital calendar). This is a great way to keep exercising your forgiveness muscles so that when the really uncomfortable situations come up, you'll be ready!

I am a certified life coach, and I know it is important to surround yourself with structure. Structure is just a fancy term for surrounding yourself with reminders of the thing(s) that you want. In the case of practicing forgiveness, you could buy a bracelet, necklace, or wristband that reminds you of forgiveness, God, the Holy Spirit, and other spiritual things. Then you could wear it every day. Some people get tattoos. (I have a tattoo of the word *Yahweh* in Hebrew on my inner right wrist to remind me to stay focused on God.) Other people may find that putting up pictures with quotes at their desks is helpful. Whatever you feel most comfortable doing at work is all good.

Having reminders, structure, digital reminders, and even daily e-mails from other Course practitioners/teachers is very helpful. But the real meat of the Course is applying it in the moment when things tend to go awry at your job.

The critical times to apply forgiveness are in the moments when things are not going well. This is easier said than done for most of us. This is the real area of practice. It's the actual moment of the *test*, whereas everything else was preparation for these moments.

It is also really important not to beat yourself up if you feel you failed the test. It's like expecting an infant learning how to walk to win a marathon after a few lessons. It's not going to happen. Because time is illusory, you can always go back and forgive the situation after the fact.

One of the greatest tools you can have (aside from following the forgiveness path) is to develop self-awareness and complete honesty about yourself. These are critical to your progression through the forgiveness steps.

There are a couple of quotes from the Course that have been really helpful in setting the stage for self-awareness. "Anger is never justified" (T-30.VI.1:1). "Do you prefer that you be right or happy?" T-29.VII.1:9).

These serve as guideposts for applying forgiveness. For some, being angry is a very natural expression of emotion, while for many others it just doesn't feel good to be around or to express. In our world of duality, there probably are times when anger feels good or needs to be released, but in the grand scheme of things, you cannot justify that it is needed because it implies fear and attacking. It is great to look into and practice forgiveness in the moment or in the past when anger arises. Anger is an excellent meter for unease in the mind and an opportunity to forgive. So are feelings of fear, guilt, depression, and sadness (among others).

When we're at work, many of us also get paid to be right. But how many of us feel it's important to bring happiness to the workplace? Imagine how productivity would increase if everyone felt loved and happy at work? It's also a reminder of another way the ego tries to trap us. We want to feel right or special and make someone else wrong (which is linked back to the original guilt we felt at the separation and the need for the ego to project that guilt outward onto other people or things).

So how do you apply forgiveness in the moment while at we are work? Here is a quick forgiveness formula.

1. Notice that you are feeling lack of peace, love, happiness, etc. (mindfulness).
2. Apply a Course phrase or thought system (interrupt the ego's process).
3. Release and join with the Holy Spirit for healing (and remembrance of who and where you really are).

When you are first learning the Course and learning to apply forgiveness, this whole process may take several seconds, or you may find that constant reminders are necessary while you are performing the functions of your job. But the more you practice forgiveness, the easier and faster it will be.

Here are some examples of applying forgiveness in work situations.

Difficult Customers

I used to work at a large bookstore in California, and it always surprised me how rude some of the customers could be when they were asking the staff for help to find books. I remember a customer came up to the information desk and just shouted the word *knees*. I was pretty new at the time, and I was surprised by the lack of connection and context. The guy seemed pretty grumpy and in a hurry.

After a few attempts of shouting the word *knees*, he gave a long exhale and said, "I'm looking for a book about knees. This is a book-store, right?" I could tell a coworker of mine was getting agitated. I just looked at him and repeated in my mind, "You are my brother in heaven." At first he looked like he was going to explode on my co-worker for showing signs of irritation. Instead he looked over at me, and in a calmer manner, he asked if we had a book that could help him.

In the end I walked him to a medical section and learned that he had knee problems and was in a lot of pain. We eventually found the right book for him, and he thanked me, a seemingly different person!

My good friend, Sheldon Jo, works at a body shop and has tons of examples of how he and his fellow employees have completely changed angry customers' experiences by practicing forgiveness or just sending out love to people or situations. They have plenty of examples of angry customers calling up. He and his team send the customer love and by the time they get to the shop, all is well! Sheldon shares great examples on our radio show, *Of Course Radio*, on BBS Radio Channel 1.

Dysfunctional Meeting Participants

Have you ever been in a meeting and thought to yourself, *This is what an insane asylum must be like*? Or at the very least been in a meeting where people were getting upset with one another? Have you been the leader or facilitator for meetings that ended up like this?

I have been in many meetings like this both as a participant and meeting leader. Here are some thoughts on practicing forgiveness in both roles.

As a participant, I would sense myself feeling anxiety or anger as certain people were speaking and then catch myself getting caught up in the drama. I would then either recognize that I created the situation or immediately repeat a Course quote like: "I thank You, Father, for Your perfect Son, and in His glory will I see my own."[7] Then in my mind I visualize the Holy Spirit coming in and healing the minds of those in the meeting.

As a meeting leader, I would start to feel anxiety, as I could tell individuals were getting upset, and I would also feel the tension between participants increasing. Depending on the situation, I may start to use the forgiveness process if other people are talking, or sometimes I will need to use the forgiveness model after I perform my duties as the meeting leader. I have led meetings where things were starting to get out of control and people were literally starting to yell at one another. Instead of sitting quietly and practicing forgiveness, I still think the best line of action is to do your job with integrity and take the time to perform forgiveness when it makes sense. I personally like to bring humor to the table, but sometimes that, too, is not appropriate. Sometimes I just need to tell people to stop! Then we can try to sort things out as rational adults. Then after the meeting, I would think back to the individuals and remember that they are spirit and ask the Holy Spirit to heal the situation.

Difficult Coworkers

I spent a couple of years as a manager in a large company, and I found it a challenge to have tough conversations with employees that needed to hear how their behavior was affecting the team. This is an area where forgiveness has made a significant positive impact on both the person I must speak with and the individuals they have to work with.

In this specific example, there was a woman who was quick to anger and would often judge her coworkers. I received several complaints and knew it was something I had to address for the sake of the individual and the greater team. Admittedly it was an issue that I was dreading to address because certain fears were running through my

---

[7] *A Course in Miracles*, T-30.IV.9:4.

mind. *What if she gets mad? What if she doesn't like me anymore? What if she goes to HR? What if nothing changes?*

Regardless of these fears, there was a stronger part of me that kept encouraging me to sit down with this person. When I brought the individual into my office, she already knew what I was going to talk to her about, but she was definitely not pleased. I let her talk for a little bit, and while I was listening, I was also applying a forgiveness phrase. I like to use one offered up in the book *Your Immortal Reality* by Gary Renard. After seeing this person for who she really was (spirit), I definitely felt more peaceful and relaxed. From what I could tell, the other person started to become more peaceful as well.

Every time I interacted with this person, I did two things. First I would say something positive to her about her contribution to the project. Then I would repeat the forgiveness thought from *Your Immortal Reality*. I'll share more of the outcome of this interaction in a later chapter.

Forgiving the Situation/Company

Since corporations are legally seen as individuals, I think it also makes sense to treat them that way in your mind. Relationship coaching will also tell you that couples, families, and companies form their own personalities and that the relationship or company becomes a person.

Since this seems to be true, then forgiveness will also work when you apply these principles to teams, projects, or companies.

This is good to practice, especially if you are surrounded by negative coworkers or the group/company is going through some tough times (layoffs, poor earnings, labor disputes, uncertainty of the future, etc.).

Here is a forgiveness method that can be used to provide healing at this level of the mind.

  – Remember that the situation or the company is simply a reflection of the greater egoic mind projecting duality into the experience.

- Offer a forgiveness thought to shift your perspective around the situation or the company. "God did not create a meaningless world. He did not create [specify the situation which is disturbing you], and so it is not real" (Lesson 14; W.pI.14.7:4–5). "God is the Love in which I forgive" (Lesson 46; W.pI.46).
- You can then either hand the situation/company over to the Holy Spirit, or you can visualize the Holy Spirit coming into the situation or company and then filling it with pure white light, which is sometimes fun. Sit with that until you start to feel peace around the situation.

There will most likely be people or situations that do not seem to be getting any better or that still suck you in and pull you out of peace. These are the really juicy forgiveness situations that may require you to put in forgiveness overtime after work. Also remember, it's not about external things around you changing, but how you are thinking and feeling within your own experience.

For colleagues or bosses that trigger you to feel out of sorts, two great lessons in the Course can help you work through these issues. Lesson 68 says, "Love holds no grievances." And lesson 69 says, "My grievances hide the light of the world in me." Both can be done as meditations/visualizations. Visualization can be a very powerful and useful tool as you practice forgiveness. It is another method of training the mind and getting your mind to shift and think with the Holy Spirit.

It might be useful to record both of these lessons and then listen to them with your eyes closed. Learn to put pauses after some of the material to give yourself an opportunity to work with the lesson and the visualizations.

Practicing forgiveness should (at the very least) naturally result in experiencing more peace in life (with the exception of ego flare-ups from time to time). (See chapter 10.) You may even see some miracles take place around you, but it isn't something that you should expect all the time.

You should hopefully have some good tools and examples to keep you going as a model of forgiveness at work. I would recommend that you start going through the Text and Workbook and pulling out quotes that really speak to you. Figure out how to either memorize some or have them handy so that you can refer to them throughout your workday.

There will definitely come days when you will wonder if this is working or not. There will be days where you don't feel like forgiving much. But in the end, forgiveness should be leading you down a very happy path.

One of the most powerful realizations I had when I was learning about the Course and forgiveness was how incredible it felt to see other people with love and compassion. When I don't remember to forgive I can feel my body tense. Then I default to judgment or fear around a person or situation. When I look at someone intending love or peace, I feel more love and peace. This may sound elementary to some of you, but what a powerful perspective to hold in the workplace. Just holding love and peace in your mind and directing it toward others returns the same to you. It may also vastly improve the work situation at the same time.

CHAPTER 7

The Holy Spirit at Work

It's safe to say that your fractured mind cannot fathom how miracles and healing occur in any situation. This is why handing things over to the Holy Spirit is so important.

1. It takes the burden and potential guilt away from you in order to make you responsible for healing and solving problems.
2. The Holy Spirit's mind is completely whole, whereas yours is not.
3. The Holy Spirit sees the bigger picture and what's better for all involved. You can only see a tiny sliver of the picture.

"The Holy Spirit atones in all of us by undoing, and thus lifts the burden you have placed in your mind. By following Him you are led back to God where you belong, and how can you find the way except by taking your brother with you?" (T-5.IV.6:1–2).

Working with the Holy Spirit is meant to be a very personal experience. Like the Course says, the Holy Spirit is your Guide, Comforter, and Healer. I also like how the ascended masters teach Gary Renard to have a more personal relationship with the Holy Spirit. They encourage him to work with Jesus Christ (they call him J) and to make that relationship personal. They take the formality out, unlike most religions. They depict Jesus as the Holy Spirit but also remind us that the Holy Spirit and Jesus have a great sense of humor with all of us "guilty bastards."

Which brings up a good point. While many students are working with the Course, they wonder how to tell the difference between the ego's voice and the Holy Spirit's voice. A few guidelines would include the following:

- The ego is always trying to compare, judge, and project everything outward, while the Holy Spirit sees everyone and everything with love and as one, perfect and whole.
- The ego will look for ways to trick you into thinking that you're better than all of the others, or if that doesn't work, it'll make you believe you're worse than all of the others. The Holy Spirit will keep reminding you that you and your brothers and sisters are all spirit.
- The ego's answers are typically complex or involve getting something from the world. The Holy Spirit's responses are simple and all about God or being back with God (not of this world).
- The ego wants you to be done with *A Course in Miracles* yesterday and will try to convince you that you are complete and done and that there's nothing left to learn. The Holy Spirit will remind you that you're done when you're done and that only God can complete the last step.
- The ego's responses will have a more masculine/aggressive feel to them, whereas the Holy Spirit's responses will feel more feminine in nature. Even the nudging around taking action will feel very gentle.

Regardless, it is important for you to develop a relationship with the Holy Spirit for yourself. To experiment and understand how you receive messages from spirit. Some people see images or words. Others can hear words. Some are feelers/intuitive. Others are able to receive input from many sources. It's important to take time and understand how you receive messages, especially from a higher source.

I have found that I can intuit/feel messages from Holy Spirit, and I tend to feel them (when I concentrate on the source) around the upper right and back portion of my head or chest. I have also learned that the women placed in my life are spiritual leaders, and when I receive suggestions from them, I know I had better listen (which was a whole cycle of forgiveness lessons for me).

When some people are working with the Holy Spirit, they like to work with visuals and imagine the traditional Christian symbol of a dove. Others imagine certain ascended masters like Jesus Christ or Mary Magdalene. Some imagine white balls of light. The symbol doesn't really matter as much as the relationship with the Holy Spirit and how you practice forgiveness in your daily life.

The late Ron Roth taught others about working with the Holy Spirit, and he would use a very simple phrase to create an immediate connection. He would say, "Holy Spirit, come." Try it. You might really like how that feels.

Developing a relationship with the Holy Spirit can be a lot of fun as well. This is a great opportunity to find some quiet time outside of work to do some meditating or visualization in order to create a connection with the Holy Spirit. Here is a quick visualization guide to do just that.

1. Get in a quiet space. Light some candles to set a mood of relaxation.
2. Get in a comfortable position (one that won't allow you to fall asleep easily) and close your eyes. Begin to relax and take a few deep breaths.
3. Imagine a white light surrounding your body and then moving all throughout your body until you are completely infused.
4. Notice if you sense or see any blocks in your body, energy field, or mind. If you do, allow the light to dissolve these blocks. Do the same if you feel any pain or discomfort.
5. Now invite the Holy Spirit in. It is important to try to not have any expectations of what this encounter should look like or feel like. Just allow the connection to happen.
6. Notice where you feel a presence. Notice if you see any colors, symbols, or figures. If you are not getting much, keep repeating, "Holy Spirit, come."

7. In your mind, ask the Holy Spirit to make its presence known to you by placing hands on your shoulder. Notice what you feel and experience.
8. Ask the Holy Spirit to perform any needed healing.
9. Ask the Holy Spirit what it most wants you to know right now.
10. Ask the Holy Spirit how to best connect on a daily basis.
11. Thank the Holy Spirit for this beautiful connection, and allow yourself to begin to remember where you are in your body.
12. Move your fingers and toes around until you feel completely grounded.
13. Slowly open your eyes.

Some people may not feel a connection the first time doing the visualization. Just enjoy taking the time to relax and making time for yourself. Just keep practicing. It may be easier if you record your own visualization and listen to it.

What will be most important is taking this relationship into the workplace. I don't just recommend only practicing forgiveness and releasing negative thoughts to the Holy Spirit. I would also recommend taking it a step further. Actually invite the Holy Spirit into your workplace as a forgiveness buddy. Visualize the Holy Spirit working with you on a daily basis. When you go into a meeting, imagine the Holy Spirit is sitting right next to you or even sitting next to the problem child of the group and sending healing thoughts.

Sometimes it's helpful to imagine you're floating above the work scene with the Holy Spirit (above the battlefield) and sending healing thoughts/light to your coworkers.

Before you start your day, Gary Renard recommends you visualize the Holy Spirit taking your hand and leading you to the gates of heaven. There you can place all of your problems or issues out on an altar for God and the Holy Spirit to take care of.

You can also do this before you start the workday or an important meeting. Just visualize being at the gates of heaven with the Holy Spirit. You can then put out people or symbols of issues that you would like help with. At the very least, you will probably feel a lot more peaceful after you do this.

As a manger, I would sometimes visualize the Holy Spirit putting His arms around someone who was having a difficult time or was visibly upset. I would not always see an outward effect on the person, but I would typically feel good for offering support to someone non-verbally. And of course, sometimes I would be prompted to follow up with people later and just see how they were doing.

CHAPTER 8

Examples of Magical Results

Even though it's probably wise not to expect certain outcomes when you are practicing forgiveness, it's exhilarating to see how the Holy Spirit can heal situations in ways you would never expect. This chapter will reveal some of the more magical and miraculous results I have experienced while I have practiced *A Course in Miracles* within the workplace.

I remember when I first came back to work at my current company in the fall of 2008. I was still riding a wave of happiness after I had been living in the Bay Area and been submerged in the Course with great friends. I was walking into work one day, and I was inviting the Holy Spirit in and visualizing light around the entire work campus. I was surrounded by people walking into work with their heads down or looking at their cell phones. I remember just looking around for anyone to make eye contact with, and then I caught the eye of a younger gentleman. He made a beeline over to me, and we started talking. I came to find out that he was a very spiritual guy and that he just felt the urge to come over and chat. I never saw him again after that, but I remember that encounter helped me realize how important it was to focus on spirituality at work as opposed to what I would normally have done. I would have compartmentalized. In the past I would never have thought to integrate my spiritual practice at work. I would have just practiced it after work. It's pretty silly, but it's funny how I can be at times.

At one point in my return, I remember having a rather difficult boss to work with. He was always upsetting people in our group or customers we would have to interact with. I felt that half of my job was performing damage control. He was also a bit of a control freak because he used to do my job and he was good at it. I remember him openly challenging me even though I knew I was technically right on a certain issue. I decided to practice Lesson 68 from the Course and imagined myself letting go of any grievances with him. I also remember feeling the urge to actually tell him I was upset with him, and I remember feeling both fear and anger at the same time. But then I immediately asked the Holy Spirit to intervene and to heal our relationship. I remember from that moment on, my boss's attitude toward me changed. He was very supportive and very complementary. Something I never would have expected. Unfortunately this change in attitude only applied to me, and he continued to upset my colleagues. Eventually I moved on to another group.

I would say my greatest challenges in the corporate world have come to me as a manager. My first management assignment was extremely stressful, and I often forgot to employ what I had learned through the Course at the beginning. I tended to beat myself up quite a bit at and I knew I needed to implement some structure in order to recover. I decided to set a meeting notice for myself first thing in the morning so that when I booted up my computer, I would take the time to either read from the Course or look at the lessons online.

This was a time at work when my R & D group was going through a process of working with an internal new customer that tended to be very heavy-handed and controlling. Morale was at an all-time low, and there were two people in particular who were at odds with my group and spent a great deal of time criticizing their work, past and present. I spent many mornings thinking about those two people and practicing forgiveness. I kept asking for guidance and help from the Holy Spirit. I noticed the more I did this, the better the relationship I was developing with both of these people.

Unfortunately my team was still feeling down about how they were being treated. I continued to forgive and to develop even better relationships with these internal customers on a physical level. At one point one of these two individuals just decided to retire. Wow! We were all really surprised. To this day I do not know the real reason he retired.

The funny thing is, the person who retired was recently hired back into our company and I have noticed my anger comes up at times when this individual speaks in meetings. I found I really needed to practice forgiveness when this person first came back. I have since been able to see this person with more tenderness and appreciation for what they bring to the table.

The second individual was a bit of a different matter. I had to have some intense one-on-one talks with this person and the effect he was having on the greater team. Unfortunately it didn't seem to faze him, and he tended to project any issues he had onto other teammates. I went as far as talking with the management team to have him removed from the project.

Things were actually lining up for that to happen when a couple of things transpired. First I was offered a job in another group, and then that individual was given a promotion.

What was really interesting was that I judged the fact that this individual was promoted to mean something had failed. When I checked back in with the team a few months after my departure, they were in a lot better spirits and said that the person who was giving them so much trouble was hardly around at all and everyone was feeling much better. Thank You, Holy Spirit! Also a lesson to not judge situations because my little mind has no idea what Holy Spirit is doing behind the scenes.

My later experience as a manager also involved a team that was a bit dysfunctional and the individuals tended to argue with one another a lot. There was one person in particular who tended to receive a lot of complaints associated whenever their name was brought up. I remember practicing forgiveness and visualizing the Holy Spirit around this person and in meetings we were all attending. I have to admit that my boss was also a great help in getting the group to work together better, and we saw huge improvements with how the team came together in meetings. However, the individual who upset people was still doing so outside of meetings.

I felt an urge to have one-on-one talks with this person, and I also noticed I had some fears around how they might react. I kept asking for the Holy Spirit to help prior to our meeting. On the day of the meeting, I could not have been more surprised. The person knew why I had called them in and openly admitted that they had issues, and were also willing to work on them. To be honest, I have never seen someone turn their behavior pattern around so quickly. Recently I received several compliments about this person and how much their attitude has improved. I am still in awe at how this person stepped up to improve their relationship with others. Another win for the Holy Spirit!

Another recent example involved trying to meet the schedule and budget on a development project. My colleagues and I were navigating through several different roadblocks we were encountering. We had issues finding resources to get some simple tooling fabricated. We then decided we needed to go outside the company to get our items fabricated. We received quotes back and submitted the numbers to senior leadership. We were basically told to "hit the showers" and find another way (namely a cheaper, faster way to go).

I noticed at first I was starting to feel some stress around the project and what to do. But luckily I remembered, "I could see peace instead of this" (W.pI.34). I let go of my need to control the situation and handed it over to the Holy Spirit. I decided to relax and stay open to any messages. Within minutes I felt an urge to go walk the shop floor and see what was available. I happened upon a shop worker whom I had known for several years. He was standing by a machine that was just implemented for use. I told him about our project, and he got really excited. He said he had plenty of time to help us and had some material we could even use for our project. In a matter of minutes, we went from no solution to an excellent solution that was going to cost us very little money. Score yet another win for the Holy Spirit!

Here is one last example of how I think the Holy Spirit has been helping out at my corporate job. I was recently assigned to lead a development project that involved people from all of the country (plus Moscow) as well as having to implement changes at an outside supplier.

The project set up looked pretty typical for my recent experiences (challenging and a high probability of ego's slamming together). To my great surprise and delight, this has been one of the most pleasant teams I have ever worked with. We have had a lot of challenges but the individuals have worked really well with each other and are always finding ways to overcome issues. I kept handing over every little issue to the Holy Spirit and have been blown away to see the results of letting Spirit be the project manager.

I cannot wait to see what He will do on the next project. Of course I'm not expecting the next project to go as well, but who knows?

I also wanted to include a couple examples of letting the Holy Spirit take over situations outside of the workplace. The first example involves dealing with the typical angry driver on the road. I grew up outside of the Detroit and driving on the road has always been a huge area of learning for me. I was taught to drive angry and aggressive. Never a good combination.

Over the years I have really worked on my attitude while driving and continue to do so to this day. I am constantly reminding myself to drive with peace in my mind and to hand over encounters to the Holy Spirit.

In a recent incident, I was driving home from work and waiting to turn right on red. There was traffic to my right cleared for left turns. A younger man had decided to make a u-turn instead of a left turn. I started to go but saw him coming and stopped. The younger man was infuriated with what I did and made some obscene gestures while screaming at me out of his window. I could feel my old programming kicking in and anger welling up. Instead I chose to remember that I created this situation (once again) and handed it over to the Holy Spirit to heal. I eventually pulled out into traffic and was behind the angry young man. He was still yelling into his rear view mirror and I just hung back and kept sending peace. Oddly enough, he turned right into a parking lot (no one was there) and I was on my way again.

More recently, my wife and I were at a comedy show in a large theater. The lights went down and the gentleman in front of us kept looking at his phone checking sports scores and the light was bothering everyone around him. I decided to try an experiment. I asked the Holy Spirit to come into the situation and in my mind I repeated, 'I would rather see peace instead of this'. Literally within minutes, the gentleman and his wife got up and left the show. Beyond coincidence considering there a couple thousands people around and the couple were the only ones to leave at that time.

I do not expect my outward situations to change so dramatically, but I do think the Holy Spirit will let you know that He is your true healing partner. Not all external circumstances will change like the examples above, but the more your mind is at peace by handing the responsibility over to the Holy Spirit, the more you will experience a happy dream.

CHAPTER 9

Workplace as a Mastery School

For many people who get into spirituality and self-help movements, there is a lot of focus on quitting your job and doing something that you love. I definitely went down this path as a life coach, but I quickly became one of the statistics of failed small-business owner.

What if it's not about doing what you love but instead about learning to love anything no matter what you are doing? That's pretty profound, and it's in alignment with the Course's point. The world doesn't matter, so why should it matter what you do or what you appear to see? It should only matter how your mind perceives the world and your brothers and sisters.

The way I see it, you can be happy no matter where you appear to be and what you appear to be doing. True mastery would say that you are happy and feel no pain no matter what.

True mastery could look like someone being thrown into prison but still maintaining an inner happiness. I would imagine that could happen by both practicing forgiveness and keeping your mind focused on God's Love. If you're going to be sitting around a lot, you might as well make good use of the illusory time.

The same can be said for your job. I know some people look at their jobs as prison sentences! So why not use that time for forgiveness instead of focusing on a different future outside of work. You can use all of the experiences you go through to forgive yourself, your coworkers, and the company on a daily basis. The funny thing is that by practicing forgiveness, you will most likely find your situation changes anyway so that you can start experiencing a happier dream.

What if you didn't work at a dream job but still felt joy, peace, and happiness all the same?

The Buddhists tell stories of enlightened monks that would be happy no matter what chores they were doing. Whether cleaning the dishes or mopping the floor, they lived in a state of happiness and connection to the source.

There are some things you could try when you have a free moment at work (or one you create) or even take a moment in a meeting that you are not running. (Make sure you are prepared if you're called on.) Here are some things I recommend you could try to advance your mastery at work.

- Imagine yourself surrounded by the love of God. It might be easier with your eyes closed, but you can try this with your eyes open in the middle of a meeting as well. Keep imagining this until you either feel a shift or see light appear.
- Imagine columns of light emanating from all of your coworkers in the room. Imagine these columns connecting into one pool of light above the room. You can also imagine that you have a column of light connecting upward as well.
- Look at people in the room (or close your eyes and imagine them) and then repeat certain forgiveness phrases from the Course or other sources (see appendix B).
- Remind yourself that this meeting or this activity is not really going on and that you and all involved are resting peacefully in heaven at this very moment.
- Pick someone from your team or project you either have had a hard time with or rarely speak to and start a conversation. See them as spirit while you are talking with them.
- Take a pause during the day, and in your mind, ask the Holy Spirit if there is someone you should speak to or if you may be needed to fulfill His plan somewhere in that moment. Wait for a response and see if you get an intuitive message, a phone call, or an e-mail. You'd be surprised how quickly and openly the Holy Spirit works!

Like I have mentioned in the earlier chapters, I have had some very wondrous experiences while I was practicing the Course at work. I have shifted from dreading days going into work to finally enjoying what I am doing at work regardless of what my job title or role is. I have been amazed that once I stopped approaching my job with one leg out the door, things seemed to really shift. I was all in and practicing my spirituality every day at work. Because of it, I feel that doors have opened up in my career that are now allowing me to live the happy dream instead of walking into a nightmare all the time.

CHAPTER 10

Why Is This So Hard?

The simple answer is that the Course states that the path is easy, but in our minds we have a belief that forgiveness leads us to hell.[8] As we learned about the metaphysics of the Course, we know that the ego is very fearful and feels guilt for appearing to separate from God, so it does not want anything to do with a true path back to God. That's why most religions have great intentions but typically go astray when they bring judgment, fear, and projection into the picture. The ego is a mastermind at distorting the truth just enough that we think we're on the right path when we actually are not.

The ego wants us to think that we are bodies and separate from one another and will do a really good job of putting people and situations in front of us that will personally trigger us and make us forget who we really are.

If you meditated in a cave for decades only thinking about God, it might be a direct path back to God. But the reality for most of us is that we are running a current script. We go to a job and have very interesting experiences. This is a perfect opportunity to practice forgiveness. If you walked around thinking everyone around you is spirit and at Home with God, you would eventually believe that about yourself as well. And in that strong belief, you would eventually just live that experience every day.

But like mastering any process, instrument, or career, it all takes practice. You are literally reprogramming your mind to stop thinking with the ego and to start thinking with the Holy Spirit. You are

---

[8] *A Course in Miracles*, T-29.II.1:4.

learning to be a true Jedi knight. To expect thinking with your ego-tistic mind to change overnight is pretty ambitious. This course is all about repetition and single-mindedness.

To be able to walk around and see everyone and everything as spirit is very challenging. This is something that ascended masters have achieved. How many ascended masters do you know? This illu-sory world sure feels and seems real to all of us, and it takes a com-pletely different mind-set to not be of this world any longer.

According to the Course, Jesus' crucifixion on the cross was meant to be a major teaching lesson. It was meant to show how a body could be tortured and killed, but the mind was still connected with the Spirit and God.

When I read *The Disappearance of the Universe*, I really resonated with how the ascended masters taught that Jesus felt absolutely no pain when he was crucified because he was completely enlightened. That makes absolute sense to me. If you are one with God in your mind and spirit, then the body stays an illusion, but the mind, now joined with the Holy Spirit and God, no longer feels or identifies with pain.

To achieve this state requires absolute single-mindedness. That takes a lot of practice.

Another reason why remembering who we are and practicing true forgiveness can be tough is that our ego mind is pretty much one big computer program. We have been programmed to think with the ego and to run from the truth. When you practice forgiveness, the Holy Spirit heals as well as reprograms your personal software suite and affects the greater system. The ego is operating one major operating system called "Guilt and Fear." Through this operating system, there are many other software programs running that look like individual people, crazy experiences, good experiences, etc. Each time a piece of software is healed at some level, it affects the greater operating system. Every moment you choose peace, love or side with the Holy Spirit is creating healing within your mind.

CHAPTER 11

Parting Thoughts

Regardless of where you are in your spiritual practices or position in a work environment, you can increase your sense of peace, joy, and happiness by practicing true forgiveness. Even if you feel really good about yourself or those around you, there are probably more ways where you can let the world start to disappear and see your brothers and sisters as spirit deserving the love of God.

Practicing forgiveness at the workplace is taking advantage of the ideal environment for truly becoming a spiritual master. If you change your perspective and realize that your main career/job is to practice the true method of forgiveness by means of *A Course in Miracles*, you will most definitely feel a change within yourself, and you may even see your external world change into a happier dream.

When you walk into your job in the mornings, just remember the basic formula for forgiveness.

1. God did not create the world you are seeing. You did when you chose to split with God.
2. Say to yourself, 'I would rather see peace and experience my true place in heaven than indulge in this illusion.'
3. Release your thoughts and what you see with your physical eyes to the Holy Spirit so that your mind can be healed.
4. Just wish love and peace to the people and situations around you. When you feel anything other than love or peace, repeat the forgiveness formula.
5. If you're feeling really down, helpless, or fearful, just completely let go of any desire to change how you feel on your

own. Just call in the Holy Spirit and say, "Holy Spirit, please heal my mind and help me see things differently. Holy Spirit, you are the great healer, and I put this situation into your hands. I'd rather experience happiness over this."

Throughout the day, practice mindfulness as best as you can and use the forgiveness thought systems that are loaded throughout *A Course in Miracles*.

Actively look to heal and be at peace with anyone at work or in your life who might create unease, anger, jealousy, or fear. Use meeting times to connect with Holy Spirit (or an ascended master of your choice) to heal troubling relationships or work situations. Remember— no job is too big for the Holy Spirit. All miracles are the same because they are simply correcting your mind to the true reality, namely that you are safe with God in heaven.

Throughout the forgiveness process, develop a deeper relationship with God, the Holy Spirit, and/or masters. Learn to understand how you receive messages from these sources. This will help you understand how to deal with situations after you have forgiven. You may be guided to move on from a situation or to sit still while you work out more issues.

But the most important things to keep in mind as you walk down the path of true forgiveness is to be gentle with yourself and to laugh at all of the craziness around you and the mistakes you will make. This certainly can be a fun and enjoyable journey!

If you made a commitment today to transform your job into a career of forgiveness, I know that you will eventually be led to a more peaceful experience. You may need to transition through some rapids from time to time, but in the end, you should feel more peace and happiness.

The journey back home to God may have some rough patches in it and may seem daunting at times, but that's just a setup. If you pause and remember that you are already at home, the mountains will begin to disappear, and you will find the strength to continue your journey in earnest.

Also remember that you are never alone, even if it appears that way because that, too, is a trick of the ego. How can you be alone when you are a loved child of God? If anything, that should be a constant companion on your journey to enlightenment.

Please feel free to use the resources listed in the appendix sections of this book to help you on your journey of living a life of secret spiritual mastery at work. Enjoy!

Course Resources

A Course in Miracles can be purchased through the Foundation for Inner Peace at http://shop.acim.org.

A Course in Miracles study group finder can be accessed at http://www.miraclecenter.org/services/study-groups.php.

Recommended *A Course in Miracles* Authors

- Busfield, Robyn: http://www.robynbusfield.com.
- Dugan, Susan: http://www.foraysinforgiveness.com/my-books.
- Hadley, Jennifer: http://jenniferhadley.com/store.
- Miller, D Patrick: http://www.fearlessbooks.com/20Years.htm.
- Mundy PhD, John: http://www.miraclesmagazine.org/#!-books/c13fx. John Mundy is the author of *Living A Course in Miracles*.
- Renard, Gary: http://www.garyrenard.com/Order.htm. Gary Renard is the author of fabulous books in which he interacts with the ascended masters Arten and Pursah and talks about all the things in *A Course in Miracles* in the books: The Disappearance of the Universe, Your Immortal Reality, and Love Has Forgotten No One. Gary also travels and teaches workshops.
- Wapnick, Ken: https://www.facim.org/bookstore. Ken Wapnick has written too many books to list here and has an outstanding selection of audio programs from past workshops. Unfortunately Ken left his body in 2014, but courses are still offered through the Foundation for *A Course in Miracles*.

- Williamson, Marianne: http://marianne.com/books. Marianne Williamson is a world-famous *A Course in Miracles* author, and she was a guest on the *Oprah Winfrey Show*.

A Course in Miracles **Workbook Lesson Resources**

- Daily lessons can be found at http://www.acim.org/Lessons/index.html.
- Workbook lesson cards can be accessed at http://shop.acim.org/collections/related-materials/products/lesson-cards.

For more information about the history of *A Course in Miracles*, please visit the Foundation for Inner Peace website at http://www.acim.org/Scribing/about_scribes.html.

Forgiveness Thought Systems to Use at Work

The enclosed thought systems are meant to reframe your mind and allow you to practice forgiveness and spirituality while you are in the workplace. You should repeat these thought systems out loud to yourself. It might be handy to have your favorite ones memorized, written in a day planner or planning app, written on your hand for the day, or displayed as reminders in other ways so that you can get into the habit of applying forgiveness and joining with God and your brothers and sisters throughout the day.

Some of the forgiveness thought systems have been made up by the author, and some are direct quotes from *A Course in Miracles*. The quotes from the Course are annotated.

When you're chatting or interacting with a coworker or when you're in a meeting with others, these statements can be used with either people you get along with or others you have difficulties with.

- "You are the Holy Son of God in Heaven and perfectly at peace."
- "Because I will to know myself, I see you as God's Son and my brother" (T-9.II.12:6).
- "You are the face of Christ. In You I am Home."
- "You are perfectly whole and innocent. Your mind is healed."
- "Light and joy and peace abide in you. Your sinlessness is guaranteed by God" (W.pI.93.11:3–4).
- "You are at Home with God in Heaven."

- "Peace, joy, and happiness reside in you. For that I am wholly grateful."
- "I choose to see my brother's sinlessness" (W.pII.335).

When you have moments alone or can spend time reminding yourself of forgiveness, you can bear these quotes in mind.

- "I am in Heaven with God, my Father."
- "The hush of Heaven holds my heart today" (W.pII.286).
- "The Son of God is my Identity" (W.pII.252).
- "I am not a body. I am free. For I am still as God created me" (W.pI.ReviewVI.3:3–5).
- "I let go and allow the Holy Spirit to guide my day."
- "Holy Spirit, come and show me how You would have me go through my day."
- "I am at Home with God, and seeing my bothers and sisters as spirit is the way to remember Home."

When you are having trouble staying positive at work (or in life) or your workplace is experiencing turbulent times, inspire yourself with the following statements:

- "I can elect to change all thoughts that hurt" (W.pII.284).
- "My holiness shines bright and clear today" (W.pII.285).
- "All fear is past and only love is here" (W.pII.293).
- "Eternal holiness abides in me" (W.pII.299)
- "Holy Spirit, come and change my mind about this situation. I would rather experience peace and happiness."
- "I can replace my feelings of depression, anxiety or worry [or my thoughts about this situation, personality or event] with peace" (W.pI.34.6:4).
- "I will my mind to experience peace and happiness now."

- "Holy Spirit, I do not want to experience this anymore. It is Yours to heal."
- "Love is what I am, and love is what I experience."

Consider these general blessings/forgiveness thoughts direct toward a group of people, a project, or a company as a whole:

- "You are collectively the Son of God, perfectly innocent and whole."
- "Holy Spirit, I do not know what all of this is for, and so I release it to You to heal and make whole."
- "This situation may seem big, but no miracle is too large for you, Holy Spirit. Please come and heal my mind of all that I think I see."
- "I will there be light. Darkness is not my will" (W.pI.73.11:2–3).
- "Beyond this world there is a world I want. I choose to see that world instead of this, for here is nothing that I really want" (W.pI.129.7:3–4).
- "I will forgive, and this will disappear" (W.pI.193.13:3).

A Course in Miracles, 3rd ed. Mill Valley, CA: Foundation for Inner Peace, 2007.

Renard, Gary. *Love Has Forgotten No One*. Carlsbad, CA: Hay House, Inc., 2013.

Renard, Gary. *The Disappearance of the Universe*. Carlsbad, CA: Hay House, Inc., 2004 .

Renard, Gary. *Love Has Forgotten No One*. 2013, Hay House, Inc. Carlsbad, CA.

Renard, Gary. *Your Immortal Reality*. Carlsbad, CA: Hay House Inc., 2006.

http://www.acim.org/Scribing/about_scribes.html; Foundation for Inner Peace. About the Scribes. Mill Valley, CA.

Wapnick, Kenneth, PhD. *The Journey Home*. Temecula, CA: Foundation for *A Course in Miracles*.